D0745656

PLANETS

KATE RIGGS

Creative Education • Creative Paperbacks

Published by Creative Education and Creative Paperbacks
P.O. Box 227, Mankato, Minnesota 56002
Creative Education and Creative Paperbacks are imprints of
The Creative Company
www.thecreativecompany.us

Design and production by Chelsey Luther
Printed in the United States of America

Photographs by Corbis (13/Ocean, 145/Ian McKinnell/Ocean, Mark Garlick/
Science Photo Library, Steven Hobbs/Stocktrek Images, Mark Garlick Words &
Pictures Ltd/Science Photo Library, NASA, Detlev van Ravenswaay/Science Photo
Library), Defense Video & Imagery Distribution System (DVIDS), deviantART
(AlmightyHighElf), Dreamstime (Diego Barucco, Oriontrail), Getty Images
(Albert Klein, Detlev van Ravenswaay, James Stevenson, VICTOR HABBICK
VISIONS), NASA (NASA/ESA/Hubble SM4 ERO Team, NASA/JPL-Caltech/STScl),
Shutterstock (soft_light), Wikipedia (Vzb83/NASA)

Library of Congress Cataloging-in-Publication Data
Riggs, Kate.
Planets / Kate Riggs.
p. cm. — (Across the universe)
Summary: A young scientist's guide to planetary bodies, including how they
interact with other elements in the universe and emphasizing how questions and
observations can lead to discovery.
Includes bibliographical references and index.
ISBN 978-1-60818-484-2 (hardcover)
ISBN 978-1-62832-084-8 (pbk)
1. Planets—Juvenile literature. 2. Solar system—Juvenile literature. I. Title.
QB602.R54 2015
523.4—dc23   2014002315

CCSS: RI.1.1, 2, 3, 4, 5, 6, 7; RI.2.1, 2, 3, 5, 6, 7, 10;
RI.3.1, 3, 5, 7, 8; RF.2.3, 4; RF.3.3

First Edition
9 8 7 6 5 4 3 2 1

Pages 20–21 "Astronomy at Home"
activity instructions adapted from
NASA Wavelength:
http://www.nasawavelength.org
/resource/nw-000-000-002-433/

TABLE OF CONTENTS

Did you know that planets are rounded objects that **orbit** a star? Scientists called astronomers study planets. The eight planets in our **solar system** are Mercury, Venus, Earth, Mars, Jupiter, Saturn, Uranus, and Neptune.

Neptune

Pluto used to be a planet. But it was renamed a **dwarf planet** in 2006.

Four of the planets are "gas giants." Jupiter, Saturn, Uranus, and Neptune are larger than the four planets closest to the sun. Mercury is the first and hottest planet. Neptune is the last and coldest planet.

Mars is known as the "Red Planet" for the color of its **atmosphere**.

All the planets were born about 4.5 billion years ago. Big rocks and other things probably crashed into each other. Even the gas giants could have rocky cores, or centers. Scientists think Jupiter's core may be the size of Earth!

The word "planet" comes from a Greek word for "wander."

Since 2004, robots called rovers have been driving around on Mars.

Astronomers study planets with **telescopes** and spacecraft. The first planet found with a telescope was Uranus. It takes 84 years for Uranus to go around the sun. The planet has 27 moons. Most of the moons are named for characters in plays written by William Shakespeare.

Uranus's biggest moons are Oberon and Titania.

Puck Miranda Ariel Umbriel Titania Oberon

Dutch astronomer Christiaan Huygens found Saturn's rings.

>

Saturn is the farthest planet we can see from Earth. People thought it was a star until the 1600s. Saturn is made mostly of gases. But its rings are made of rock and ice.

Earth orbits the sun in 365 days.

Earth is the only planet we know of that has living things. We are close enough to the sun to get heat and light. We are not so far away that all our water turns to ice.

-290 °F

800 °F

Earth

80 °F

Tell someone what you know about planets! What else can you discover?

⌄

Sun

Venus

Mars

Earth

Mercury

Jupiter

Uranus

Saturn

Neptune

Main Asteroid Belt

SOLAR SYSTEM TO SCALE

— What you need —

3 pounds Play-Doh or clay

— What you do —

1 Make 10 equal-sized balls using all the Play-Doh.

2 Combine six of the balls to make Jupiter.

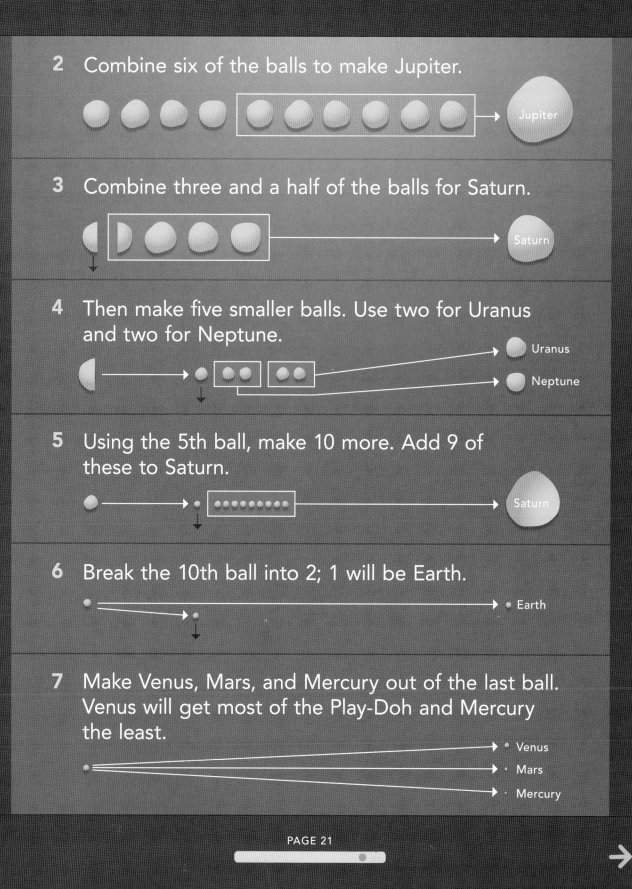

3 Combine three and a half of the balls for Saturn.

4 Then make five smaller balls. Use two for Uranus and two for Neptune.

Uranus

Neptune

5 Using the 5th ball, make 10 more. Add 9 of these to Saturn.

Saturn

6 Break the 10th ball into 2; 1 will be Earth.

Earth

7 Make Venus, Mars, and Mercury out of the last ball. Venus will get most of the Play-Doh and Mercury the least.

Venus

Mars

Mercury

GLOSSARY

	atmosphere	the gases, or air, surrounding Earth
	dwarf planet	a body that orbits the sun but is smaller than the planets
	orbit	the path a planet, moon, or other object takes around something else in outer space
	solar system	the sun, the planets, and their moons
	telescopes	viewing tools that make objects that are far away appear closer

READ MORE

Sexton, Colleen. *The Solar System.*
Minneapolis: Bellwether Media, 2010.

Zobel, Derek. *Jupiter.*
Minneapolis: Bellwether Media, 2010.

WEBSITES

NASA Jet Propulsion Laboratory—Kids
http://www.jpl.nasa.gov/kids/index.cfm
Play a planetary game or do a space-related activity.

Pluto's Secret
*http://kids.nationalgeographic.com/kids/games
/actiongames/plutos-secret/*
Explore the solar system, and find out more about
the planets!

Note: Every effort has been made to ensure that the websites listed above are suitable for children; that they have educational value, and that they contain no inappropriate material. However, because of the nature of the Internet, it is impossible to guarantee that these sites will remain active indefinitely or that their contents will not be altered.

INDEX